So Many Animals!

So Many Animals!

A Child's Book of Poetry

Edited by M.R. Street

Turtle Cove Press
1837 Easton Forest Drive • Tallahassee, FL 32317
OR 2501 Surf Road • Ochlockonee Bay, FL 32346
T: 850.566.8675 • E: editor@turtlecovepress.com
https://www.turtlecovepress.com

ISBN: 978-1947536142
Library of Congress Control Number: 2022944955

For Parents and Educators

Susan Koehler, M.S., Ed.
Author and Educator

Congratulations! You have discovered a delightful anthology of poems to share with a child in your life. This rhythmic and imaginative collection has the power to provide equal measures of joy and learning.

For the young child, poetry is fun and accessible. Passages are brief, the layout is easy for young eyes to absorb, and the beauty of language is on full display. Poetry provides practice with early literacy skills, promotes engagement, and creates a positive emotional climate around reading and language.

To make the most of developing early literacy skills, consider the following:

- Reinforce the speech-to-print connection by pointing to the text while reading aloud.
- Practice phonemic awareness by omitting rhymes and allowing the child to predict the rhyming word.
- Model fluency by reading aloud with rhythm and expression.
- Practice echo-reading by having the child repeat each line of poetry, mimicking your rhythm and inflection.
- Read the poems again and again! Repeated readings help children develop word recognition, comprehension, and fluency.
- Find organic opportunities to imitate the rhyme, rhythm, and word play found in these poems.
- Allow the child to engage with the text by coloring illustrations and adding original flourishes. (Blank pages are included for children to add their own creations!)
- Encourage the child to extend favorite poems by memorizing and acting them out, creating complementary art, and writing their own poetry.
- Develop higher order thinking by asking open-ended questions.
- Introduce the child to literary devices like alliteration, onomatopoeia, and figurative language.

Use this anthology as a springboard for learning, but above all else, allow it to be a catalyst for joy. While poetry provides a fertile field for literacy development, the positive emotional climate you create as you share these poems will remain with the child for a lifetime!

Susan Koehler is a veteran educator and the author of two award-winning middle-grade novels, **Dahlia in Bloom,** *a Kirkus Reviews Best of 2019 historical fiction selection with a starred review from Kirkus, and* **Nobody Kills Uncle Buster and Gets Away with It,** *a contemporary mystery described as "exciting, poignant, and full of heart."*

Table of Contents

Birds

Bluebird Free
Margaret Simon

Come with me,
I'm bluebird free!
Sing *tu-a-wee*
tu-a-wee
on the tiptop
of the cypress tree.

Come with me,
I'm bluebird free!
With azure wings,
I'm feathered glee.
I hide in old
woodpecker's tree.

Come with me,
I'm bluebird free!
Pick a berry
sweet as can be
from a swampy
blackgum tree.

Come with me!

Birds!
Marzieh A. Ali

Unlike me,

birds don't need a plane to fly.

Unlike me,

birds even eat for free.

Unlike me,

birds poop anywhere… not I!

I think I'm better off

being me!

When Ostrich Gets an Itch

Irene Latham

When Ostrich
gets an itch
his feathers
start to twitch.

He hitches up
his wings
and buries his head
in a ditch.

And that's when
Ostrich gets
bewitched:

his world flips,
itch by itch
by itch.

Sky? Earth?

When Ostrich
gets an itch
he can't tell which
is which.

Robin Red Breast
Dean Flowerfield

I see a Robin Red Breast

perched in yonder tree

and if I softly call to her

perhaps she'll sing to me.

Robin, Robin Red Breast

first bird of the spring

fly down from the tree top

and let me hear you sing.

Robin opens up her beak

And sings a cheerful song

I have a song inside me, too

And so I sing along

Penguin
Rachel Jacobsen

I'm a little penguin
Living in the snow

I search for friends
Everywhere I go

I'm a little penguin
Black and white

I see the stars
When I go to bed at night

I'm a little penguin
With many places to go

Fish and Reptiles

The Goldfish Bowl
Dean Flowerfield

I stared into my goldfish bowl

to see what I could see.

Deep within those waters blue,

I'd see a whale and tuna too.

Deep within those waters white,

I'd see an eel and octopus fight.

Deep within those waters green,

I'd see a hundred-foot submarine.

I stared into my goldfish bowl

to see what I could see.

But all I saw were goldfish

staring back at me.

Turtles and Gators

Margaret Simon

Turtles and gators
 amble
    in awkward strides
 scramble
    in tough-skinned boots.
Together they toe-tap,

B^um^p
B_ounce

B_o ^ogⁱ e

on a wayward log.
S t r e t c h i n g   for warm sun,
              P
Chins   U
Silent shifters.
    Swampy tricksters.
Duckweed fishers.
    Gators and turtles

    T
        u
    m
        b
    l
        e
        together.

16

Song of the Turtle Mother
M.R. Street

Her head is weary, her travels long

This is the Turtle Mother's Song

She's traveled far this shore to reach

She pushes onward up the beach

She digs a nest and lays a clutch

Of moon-shaped eggs that mean so much

The baby turtles snug within

Will hatch and then their travels begin

Now the mother leaves the shore

Returning to the waves once more

Though she is tired, her will is strong

This is the Turtle Mother's Song.

Forest

Critters

Okapi
M.R. Street

Off the beaten path, Mama

Keeps hidden in the forest shadows.

A long tongue reaches behind

Pink, new-born ears of her

Infant calf ~ Wake Up! Dinner Time!

This poem is an acrostic. The first letter of each line spells the animal's name.

What the Sloth Knows
Michelle Kogan

Movement s l o o o w and graceful,

sleeping almost all day long.

Munching our meals in mangrove trees—

Where we feel safe and where we belong.

We three-toed pygmies are critically endangered—

No trees — No habitat for me.

I want to hang out on Isla Escudo,

and go for a swim with my family.

Seasons of the Fox
M.R. Street

May: Pre-dawn, foggy

A skinny silhouette stops

Sniffs the air, dissolves

Fox, where have you gone

Disappeared with Summer's heat

On silent, silver feet

Wrapped in Autumn-orange

Black eyes keep watch on three kits

Searching for food bits

Leave Winter's warm den

Find a rabbit or a mouse

Bring back to the house

Spring brings rain, berries

Food is plentiful again

For skinny foxes

This poem is a Go-Ku *(a chain of five Haiku).*

Fall Bunnies
Michelle Kogan

Backyard fall bunnies

nibbling my berries,

begin billowing out

their bristly fur coats,

preparing for winter.

Lions
and Tigers
and Bears

Tiger Talk Triolet

Irene Latham

When tiger's tail begins to flick

she's roaring with her muscles:

Go away, quick!

When tiger's tail begins to flick,

giving her space is the trick.

Notice how your heart rustles

when tiger's tail begins to flick?

Tiger's not the only one

who's roaring with her muscles.

This poem is a triolet. *It follows the rhyme scheme*
ABaAabAB *(but with an extra line):*

A (first line)
B (second line)
a (rhymes with the first line)
A (first line repeated)
a (rhymes with the first line)
b (rhymes with the second line)
A (first line repeated)
B (second line repeated)

The Bears on the Stairs
Adrian Fogelin

There is a place at the top of the stairs,
that's a favorite haunt of night-time bears.
They park their butts so fuzzy and wide,
two across and side-by-side.

Sis and I sleep unawares,
guarded by the bears on the stairs.
Lulled by the music of grunt, rustle, groan,
we sleep secure; we are not alone.

And we dream of bears in tutus pink,
not real-life bears that snuffle and stink.
And the bears on the stairs squint into the dark,
the downstairs clock ticks, the neighbors' dogs bark.

The bears, impassive, stoic, and stout,
breathe in the night, and huff morning out.
And as first light filters through balusters white,
the nighttime bears shimmer, then vanish from sight.

But when night falls again and day flickers out,
the click of hard toenails, the damp of a snout,
the flump of butts furry, the breath tinged with trout,
tell young sleepers, you're safe, the bears are about.

Lion

M.R. Street

Lying in wait, patiently

In the tawny grass, unseen,

Only her tail twitches. She is

Nature's queen.

This poem is an acrostic. The first letter of each line spells the animal's name.

Black Bear Takes a Walk
Debra Friedland Katz

On a sunny, summer's day
A curious black bear went astray.
Instead of left, the bear turned right,
Now her woods were not in sight.

She found herself on a city street,
Propelled by four big bear-clawed feet
Past rows of houses, block by block,
Where wide-eyed neighbors stood in shock.

Past a church, a bank, a store,
Black bear walked and walked some more.
Shoppers pointed, "Look, a bear!"
Some ran away, some stopped to stare.

Cars slowed down; drivers gawked.
Still the bear just walked and walked.
The bear turned left, then left again.
Heading back to her black bear den.

She walked through quiet neighborhoods,
She walked until she reached her woods.
Black bear settled on the forest ground,
Familiar trees pressed all around.

That evening families talked and talked
About the bear that walked and walked.

Snow Tiger
Michelle Kogan

listen for tiger's

footsteps, if you can't hear them

shh... listen harder

This poem is a Haiku. *It has three lines with 5, 7, and 5 syllables.*

Dogs and Cats

Cat Hat
J.G. Annino

When Ginger Kitty is all mellow

A sleepy lappy melty fellow,

I gently place

My kitty dear,

And so

I wear him

Ear to ear.

Mr. Jaws
Adrian Fogelin

I like dogs, except for one
who lives in the apartment next door.
I see him on the elevator as we ride
down to the ground floor.

His owner's tied to him with a string,
a flimsy-skinny-stretchy thing.
The guy is old, his arm a twig
and that dog of his is mighty big,

with stick-out teeth, he's slobbery too.
He growls as he drools on my left shoe.
Now the dog's rumbling a gravelly threat,
and we're nowhere near the ground floor yet.

Mr. Jaws is one big mutt.
I'm sure he'd like to bite my butt.
The old guy says he's sweet as pie.
I swallow hard and ask him why

he calls his sweetie-dog Mr. Jaws.
The old man smiles and says, "Because,
an old fart like me needs protection.
Sweetie gives the wrong impression."

Three Wild Cats
Irene Latham

Three wild cats
with October eyes—
they watch
they hunt
they hypnotize.

I see three cats.
They see me.
Which of us
will be first to flee?

Surprise!

Three wild cats
with October eyes—
they rub
they purr.
We harmonize.

Farm Animals

Blue Ox
Linda Mitchell

Today, I wear my blue coat

with the red starburst flowers

I'll sip tea with Billy-goat

Today, I wear my blue coat

and nibble cakes of sweet oats

Even if there are rain showers

Today, I wear my blue coat

with the red starburst flowers.

This poem is a triolet. *It follows the rhyme scheme ABaAabAB.*

A Dream of Sheep
Irene Latham

Sometimes I think
a sheep

has the life
meant for me:

how untroubled
the days

in the shade
of this old tree.

I like their wooly coats,
the way they bleat

and how they eat
whenever they please.

Yes, I should have been
a sheep.

But then who—
or what—

would have been me?

My Calf, My Very Happy Sunlight
Linda Mitchell

I know your voice

since you rubbed me down

with hay and song

good boy

strong boy

my boy.

I grew and grew

with your constant call

to food

to work

to rest

My bell sings back

each *li* we walk,

My friend

My farmer

My very happy sunlight.

Goat Games
Anonymous

Toby and Watson
Would like you to know
They have lots of fun
Wherever they go

They like munching bananas
For a special treat
They can be a bit messy
With the treats that they eat

They think they are babies
Who fit in my lap
When they were little
They'd cuddle up for a nap

Now they are big
They climb mountains and trees
And when it is hot
They enjoy a cool breeze

Toby and Watson
Would like you to know
You should always have fun
Wherever you go!

Insects, Arachnids, and Other Critters

Honey Bee
M.R. Street

Honey bee, honey bee

You fly around for hours

Honey bee, honey bee

Looking for the perfect flowers

Honey bee, honey bee

You have magic powers

You make golden honey

From those perfect flowers

Monarch Enchantment
Michelle Kogan

Hey monarch butterfly

Whenever I see you a smile rolls by

and my whole spirit soars

To a place way up high

where wonder catches dreams

in the twinkling of an eye.

Arachnophobia
Adrian Fogelin

Spiders are NOT scary.
Nor are they insects either.
Spiders are arachnids.
Now give your fear a breather.

But what about the poison ones?
They're few and far between.
It's more likely that an asteroid
Will conk you on the bean.

Arachnophobia's the fancy name
for the fear that makes you scream,
But once you learn about spiders
They're not as scary as they seem.

Spiders are like ninjas.
They're stealthy and carnivorous.
But you're not on their menu
They're not THAT omnivorous.

Night Artists
Buffy Silverman

Fireflies paint

the midsummer's night.

Windows are washed

with splashes of light

with flashes of green

with brushstrokes in flight.

Ghost Crab
Ann Morrow

I'm not afraid of those ghosts on the beach,

even though their black, beady eyes follow my every move;

even though their eight legs carry them

through the darkness

faster than my two legs can.

I'm not afraid of those ghosts on the beach,

even though they can zip down into burrows without a sound;

even though their sand-colored bodies

seem to melt away

until they disappear completely.

No, I'm not afraid of those ghosts on the beach.

Those sharp eyes watch for danger; those eight legs run to safety;

those sand-colored bodies hide them, in plain sight,

from something really scary –

me!

Haiku
Rachel Jacobsen

Buzzing by the tree

Smiling wide and full of glee

Yellow bumblebee

This poem is a Haiku. *It has three lines with 5, 7, and 5 syllables.*

Spider's Song
Buffy Silverman

Spin, spin, spin your silk,

with your spinneret.

Toss a line across a vine.

Build your dinner net.

Trap, trap, trap your prize,

wrap it, then attack.

Bite a fly and suck it dry.

Slurp your favorite snack.

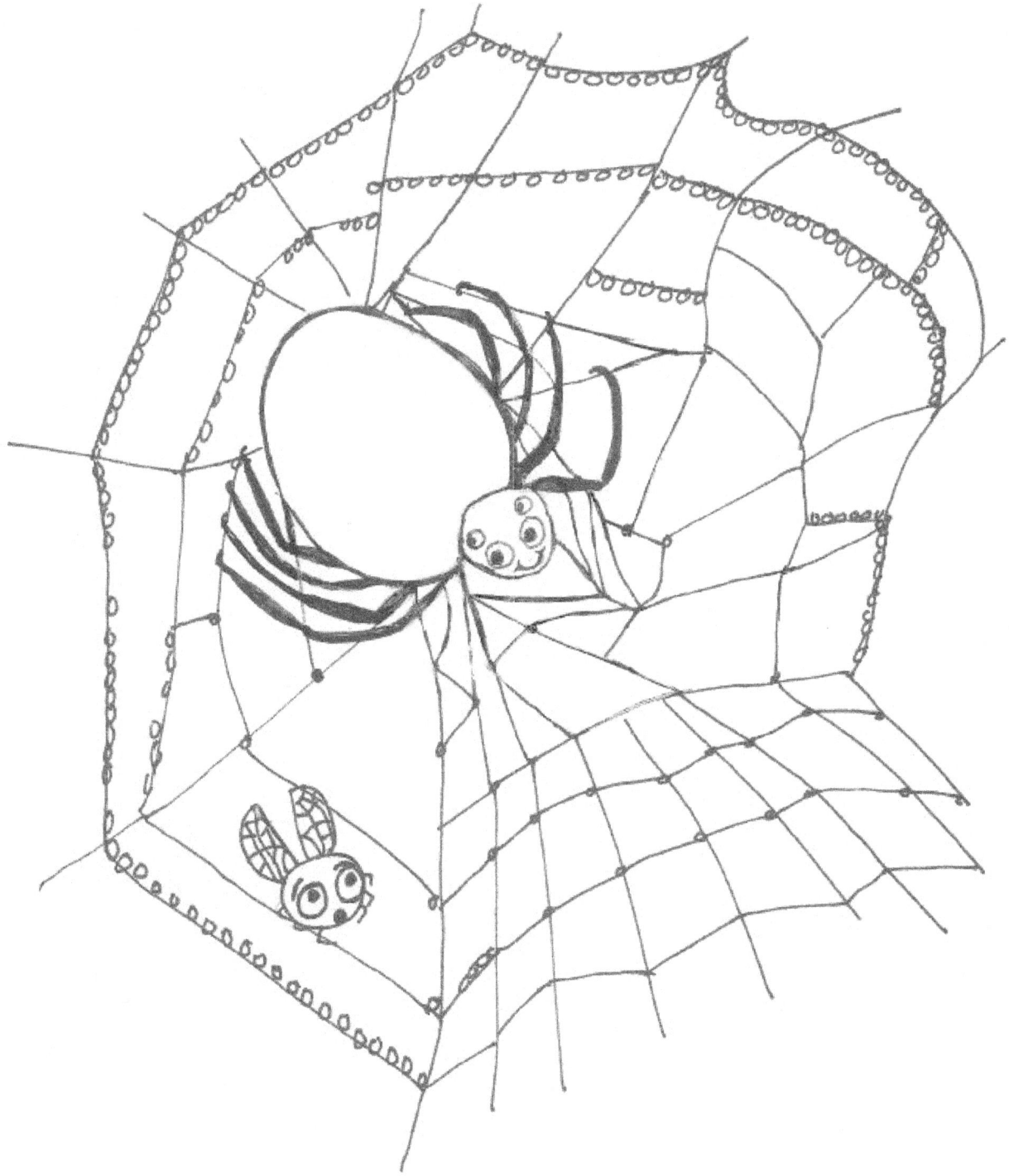

So Many Animals!

My Garden
Nick Wynne

There are many creatures in my garden,

Birds, black snakes, butterflies, bees, and moles,

They all have long scientific names,

But I call them Bill, Fred, Grace Ann, and such,

Because we're friends…

Heron's Home
Michelle Kogan

My habitat's in Caldwell Pond

by bullfrogs, ducks, and butterflies.

I fish, I fly, not far beyond

my habitat's in Caldwell Pond.

Don't get too close, sit by that frond

or *SKEOW* you'll soon hear my cries–

My habitat's in Caldwell Pond

by bullfrogs, ducks, and butterflies.

This poem is a triolet. *It follows the rhyme scheme ABaAabAB.*

Spider's Eye View
Debra Friedland Katz

Autumn leaves, brilliant red,

Surrounding spider in her web.

High up in a maple tree

Spider sees what she can see.

On the ground beneath the tree

Spider spies a rusted key.

Across the road a rabbit hops,

Heading for a field of crops.

She spots three frogs beside a pond,

One frog croaks, and two respond.

Orange pumpkins dot the scene

Just in time for Halloween.

Chimney smoke rising tall,

One curious spider sees it all.

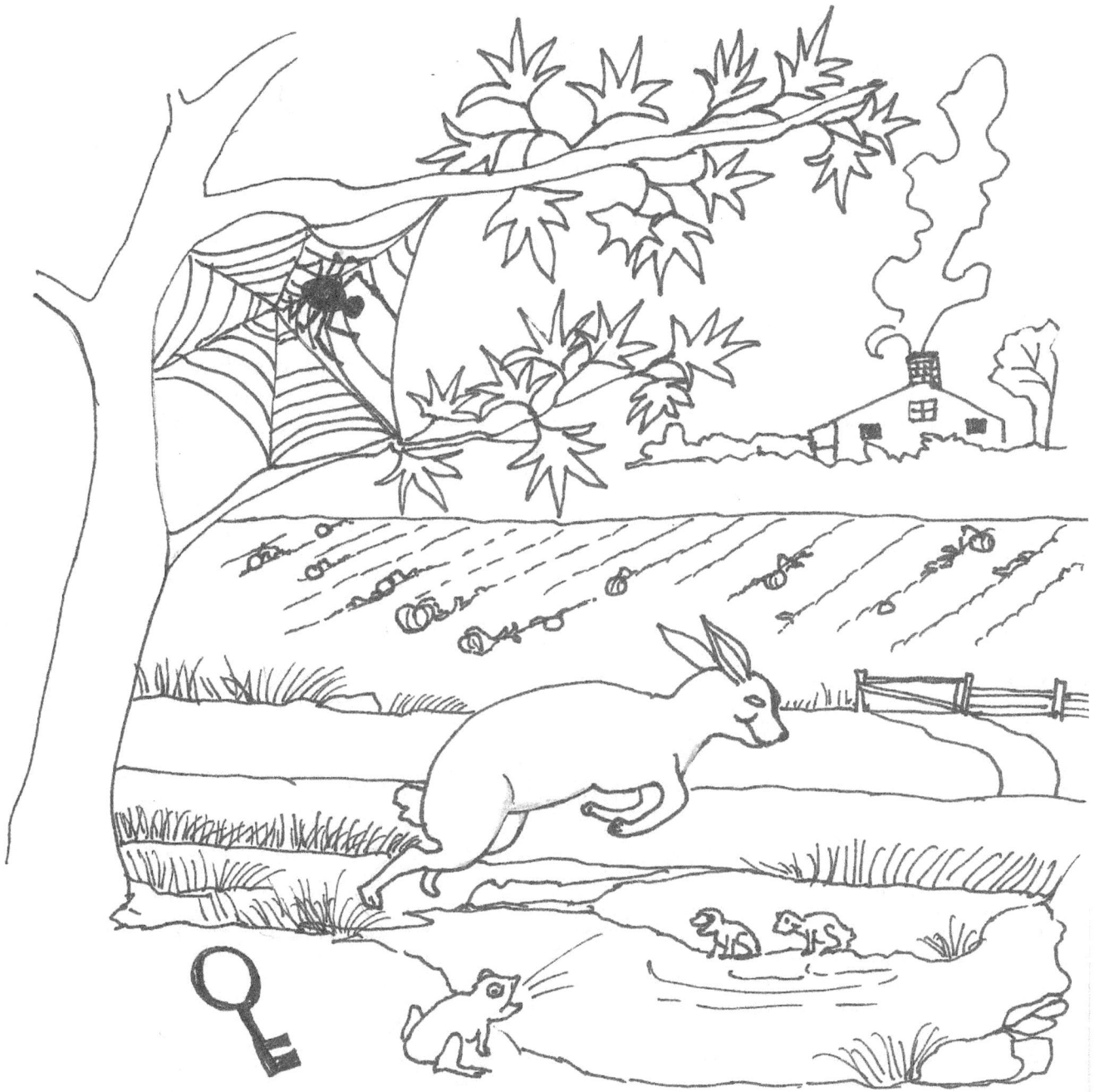

Rainbow Colors
Rachel Jacobsen

Red is for a cardinal, high in the tree

Orange is for a tiger, happy as can be

Yellow is for a duck, swimming in a pond

Green is for a grasshopper, humming on the lawn

Blue is for a dolphin, swimming in the sea

Purple is for an octopus, who is smart as can be

There are so many beautiful colors in the world around me!

Welcome Home
Ann Morrow

When gopher tortoise wants to rest
or escape the heat and cold,
it crawls into its sandy home,
a long, dark burrow,
buried deep.

But what does it do when snake slips in,
or skunk, or mouse or frog?
No door, no guard to keep them out
of that long, dark burrow,
buried deep.

I wonder if it's noisy there,
with hisses, growls and croaks.
Or do they settle without a fuss
in that long, dark burrow,
buried deep.

How wonderful to have a home
that shelters such a crowd.
A safe retreat from fires and storms,
a long, dark burrow
buried deep.

Animals all around
J.G. Annino

Sheep, sparrow, squirrel, snail.

So many animals on the trail.

Giraffe, bear, ostrich, moose.

So many animals running loose.

Camel, cricket, cardinal, crab.

So many animals, never drab.

Gorilla, owl, raccoon, monkey.

So many animals love a tree.

Look left, look right, look up and down.

So many animals, all around.

This Is My Poem
The title of my poem is

_____

My name is

_____

(Write Your Poem Here)

_____

_____

_____

_____

_____

_____

_____

_____

This Is My Illustration
(Draw a picture that shows what your poem is about)

About the Authors

Marzieh A. Ali. Raised between the bustling cities of Dubai, U.A.E., and Karachi, Pakistan, Marzieh Ali loves baking, reading, samosas, and her colorful collection of dupattas. She is a member of the Society of Children's Book Writers and Illustrators and is a lifelong learner. She runs a kid lit review group on Facebook, and blogs about her author journey and life in Pakistan. You can find her at marziehabbas.com.

J.G. Annino. Three moose, three bears, fox, monkeys, squirrels, two bobcats, butterflies, birds of shore, woods, mountains, meadows and rainforest, have crossed paths in the wild with J.G. *She Sang Promise, The Story of Betty Mae Jumper*, is her book about a leader who, among many accomplishments, also wrestled alligators.

Anonymous lives on a small farm in the Florida Panhandle with an array of animals. Her poem was inspired by her goats, Toby and Watson.

Dean Flowerfield (aka David Blumenfeld) is an emeritus philosophy professor and former associate dean who writes nonfiction, humor and children's literature. His recent publications appear in *Best New True Crime Stories: Well-Mannered Crooks, Rogues & Criminals*; *Mono.*; *Beyond Words*; *Balloons Lit. Journal*; *The Caterpillar*; *the other side of hope*; *Sport Literate*; *Better Than Starbucks*; *Smarty Pants*; *Drunk Monkeys*; *The 3rd Act*; *Holyflea!*; *The Parliament*; *Bloom*; and *The Dirigible Balloon*.

Adrian Fogelin has lived in two worlds for most of her life: the so-called real world and the world of fiction. She is the author of nine middle grade novels all published by Peachtree Publishers of Atlanta. Her works have been translated into many other languages and won numerous awards. Her first published novel, *Crossing Jordan* has enjoyed incarnations as a "One Voice" book-on-tape, a musical, and, most recently a dramatic production by Tallahassee's Young Actors Theater. She has taught numerous creative writing classes for writers of diverse ages and leads annual writer's retreats. In addition to teaching and writing she has edited a long list of titles across a wide range of genres.

Rachel Jacobsen is from sunny South Florida. She spends her days teaching children how to communicate as a pediatric speech-language pathologist. Rachel enjoys listening to podcasts in her car, worshipping her espresso machine, and attempting to teach her cat, Simba, tricks. This is her first-time writing poetry.

Debra Friedland Katz is a speech-language pathologist and a freelance writer. Her short stories, poems and nonfiction have been published in *Highlights for Children, Faces, Ladybug,* and *Story Friends* magazines.

Michelle Kogan's writing and art grow from nature and humanity. She's a poet, writer, artist, and instructor; semi-finalist for Poet's Billow 2021 Bermuda Triangle; Silver Birch Press' Prime Mover series; and anthologies 10 •10 POETRY ANTHOLOGY, Imperfect I–II, and The Best of Today's Little Ditty I–III. Visit her at www.michellekogan.com and www.moreart4all.wordpress.com.

Irene Latham is a grateful creator of many novels, poetry collections, and picture books, including the coauthored *Can I Touch Your Hair? Poems of Race, Mistakes, and Friendship*, which earned a Charlotte Huck Honor, and *The Cat Man of Aleppo*, which won a Caldecott Honor. Irene lives on a lake in rural Alabama.

Linda Mitchell is a family girl, Middle School Librarian, creative, curious, and she loves to learn! She's often found writing at O'dark-thirty at the kitchen table with her cat or dabbling in mixed media collage at the end of the day in her basement. *Blue Ox* is the author's interpretation of a painting called *Blue Ox*, by Ukranian artist Maria Primachenko.

Ann Morrow. Through her writing, Florida author Ann Morrow loves to explore the special bond children have with the natural world. She has published numerous articles, essays and poems.

Buffy Silverman's fascination with nature inspires much of her writing. Her most recent book, *On a Snow-Melting Day: Seeking Signs of Spring,* was an NCTE (National Council of Teachers of English) 2021 Notable Poetry Book. A companion book, *On a Gold-Blooming Day: Finding Fall Treasures,* launches in fall, 2022. Visit her at www.buffysilverman.com.

Margaret Simon lives with her husband on the Bayou Teche in New Iberia, LA which inspires her writing every day. She's been teaching for 35 years, most recently in elementary gifted with a Masters and National Boards Certification in literacy for young children. Her poems for children have been published in anthologies by Pomelo Books and

National Geographic. She is a member of the Society for Children's Book Writers and Illustrators and writes a blog regularly at reflectionsontheteche.com.

M.R. Street is an author and publisher based in Tallahassee and Ochlockonee Bay, FL. She enjoys reading, writing, photography, and making art. She has a beautiful view of the Bay as she works on projects on her computer, but the scenery and wildlife are often very distracting! Contact her at https://www.turtlecovepress.com.

Nick Wynne is a native of McRae, Georgia. He taught at Southern Technical Institute, the University of South Alabama, and the University of South Florida. He is the Executive Director Emeritus of The Florida Historical Society and is the author or co-author of more than 25 books. He lives in Rockledge, Florida, with his wife, Debra.

www.ingramcontent.com/pod-product-compliance
Lightning Source LLC
Chambersburg PA
CBHW080534090426
42733CB00015B/2588